American
Curl Cats

ABDO
Publishing Company

A Buddy Book
by
Julie Murray

VISIT US AT
www.abdopub.com

Published by Buddy Books, an imprint of ABDO Publishing Company, 4940 Viking Drive, Suite 622, Edina, Minnesota 55435. Copyright © 2005 by Abdo Consulting Group, Inc. International copyrights reserved in all countries. No part of this book may be reproduced in any form without written permission from the publisher.

Printed in the United States.

Edited by: Christy DeVillier
Contributing Editors: Matt Ray, Michael P. Goecke
Graphic Design: Maria Hosley
Image Research: Deborah Coldiron
Photographs: Chanan, Corel, Eyewire Inc., Helmi, Photospin, Procurl Harem

Library of Congress Cataloging-in-Publication Data

Murray, Julie, 1969-
   American curl cats/Julie Murray.
       p. cm. — (Animal kingdom. Set II)
   Includes bibliographical references and index.
   Contents: Cats — American curl cats — What they're like — What they look like — Senses — Care — Food — Kittens — Buying a kitten.
   ISBN 1-59197-301-5
       1. American curl cat—Juvenile literature. [1. American curl cat. 2. Cats.] I. Title.

SF449.A44M87 2003
636.8'3—dc21

                                                             2002038542

Contents

Domestic Cats

Domestic cats are closely related to wild cats. All cats belong to a group called Felidae. Like wild cats, domestic cats have hunting skills. They can catch and kill mice, birds, and other small animals.

There are many kinds
of domestic cats.

The Egyptians were the first people to tame cats. They brought cats indoors to kill rats and other pests. This happened about 5,000 years ago. Today, people around the world keep domestic cats as pets.

Many people have pet cats.

American Curl Cats

There are about 40 breeds of domestic cats. A few of these breeds are Siamese, Manx, and Russian blue. Another cat breed is the American curl.

A Siamese cat (left) and a Manx cat (right).

One day in 1981, a family found a cat near their home in Lakewood, California. This longhaired cat had ears that curled back. The family kept the cat and called her Shulamith. She was one of the first American curl cats.

Shulamith had kittens. Her kittens had curled ears, too. Over the years, more and more cats like Shulamith were born. People began showing these curly eared cats at cat shows. This is how the American curl breed got started.

Shulamith was a black cat
with curled ears like this cat.

What They Look Like

American curl cats are named for their curled ears. They are medium-sized cats. Adult males may weigh as much as 10 pounds (5 kg). Females are smaller.

American curl cats can have long hair or short hair. They may have different colors and markings.

American curl cats have ears that curl back.

What They Are Like

American curl cats are great family pets. They are playful and friendly. American curl cats get along well with children and other cats.

American curl cats enjoy spending time with people. Some follow their owners around. They like sleeping on a person's lap. These cats may sleep under the covers with their owners, too.

American curl cats
are great pets.

Care

Cats need food and fresh water every day. Cats also need a litter box. It should be cleaned every day.

House cats need a litter box.

Cats lick themselves to stay clean. This is called grooming. It is a good idea to brush your cat, too. Brushing removes dead hair that could lead to hair balls.

Like all cats, American curls will scratch things. Owners can trim their cat's claws. They can also train their cats to use scratching posts.

A special brush for cats.

Why Cats Scratch

Cat experts say scratching is a natural thing for cats to do. Cats scratch to:

- ❏ shed the outside layer of their growing claws
- ❏ leave their mark and their scent behind
- ❏ get attention

It is natural for cats
to scratch things.

Kittens

Baby cats are called kittens. As many as six kittens may be born in a litter. American curl kittens are born with straight ears. Their ears begin curling after about three days.

American curl kittens

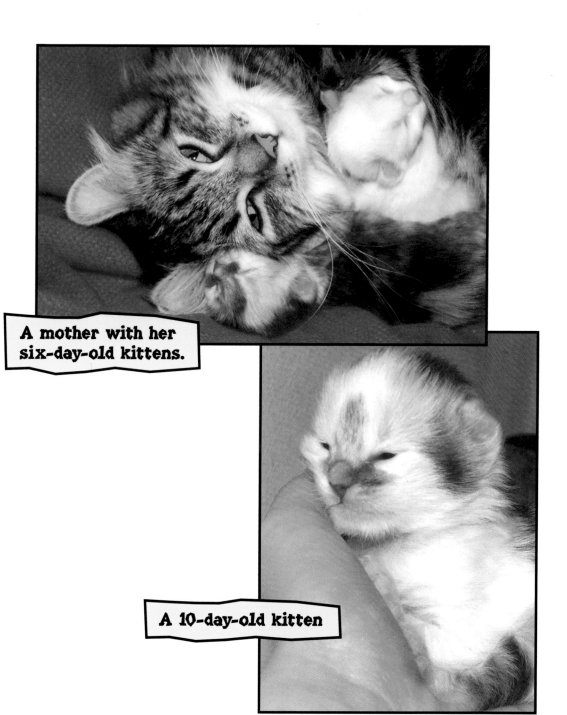

A mother with her six-day-old kittens.

A 10-day-old kitten

19

This five-week-old kitten can see and walk around.

A newborn kitten is blind and helpless. It stays close to its mother and drinks her milk. After a few weeks, a kitten can see and stand on its own. It can run and play at seven weeks old.

Kittens grow quickly.

A kitten should not leave its mother before it is 12 weeks old. It takes six to eight months for kittens to become adult cats. A healthy cat can live for 20 years.

American curl cats are lovable pets.

Important Words

breed a special group of cats. Cats of the same breed look alike.

domestic cats tame cats that make great pets.

groom to clean and care for.

hair ball hair that collects in a cat's stomach after grooming.

litter the group of kittens born at one time.

litter box a place for house cats to leave their waste.

Web Sites

To learn more about American curl cats, visit ABDO Publishing Company on the World Wide Web. Web sites about American curl cats are featured on our Book Links page. These links are routinely monitored and updated to provide the most current information available.

www.abdopub.com

Index